Starlight Sentinels

Sage Woods

To all young explorers of the starlit skies,

May your curiosity always be as boundless as the universe,

and your dreams as luminous as the stars.

This adventure is for you

may it inspire you to reach for the cosmos and discover the wonders that await.

With all the stars in the sky,

Sage

STARLIGHT SENTINELS

Book Cover by Tukotuku Publishing

Illustrations by Tukotuku Publishing

First edition 2024

Print 978-1-991306-77-7
Ebook 978-1-991306-78-4

CONTENTS

Starlight Sentinels

Welcome to the wondrous world of the Starlight Sentinels, a group of young heroes from all corners of our planet, chosen not just for their courage but for their curiosity about the cosmos. This isn't just any team; it's a special crew tasked with exploring and safeguarding the mysteries of the universe. Are you ready to journey across the stars with them? Strap in, because the adventure starts now!

Once upon a time, under the same starry sky where you've probably wished upon a twinkling star, five kids from different parts of the world watched the night unfold. They were like any other kids, filled with dreams and a love for adventure. Little did they know, their love for the stars above was about to take them on the biggest adventure of their lives.

In a hidden corner of the world, there's a secret observatory perched on the highest peak. This isn't just any observatory; it's the headquarters of the Starlight Sentinels. It was here, under the luminous moonlight, that our heroes met for the first time, brought together by a mysterious force known only as "The Celestial Stream." This force is said to flow through the universe, connecting all things celestial with the heartbeats of these chosen guardians.

Our team includes Leo from Brazil, who can chart stars faster than you can blink; Jin from Korea, with a mind as sharp as a comet's tail; Sarah from Kenya, who dances with the Northern Lights; Amir from Egypt, who speaks in cosmic codes; and Mia from Canada, who can hear the whispers of the moon. Together, they form a circle of friends bound by their destiny to protect the wonders of the night sky.

The Starlight Sentinels' first mission? To solve the riddle of the disappearing comets. Every hundred years, a comet named Halley returns to grace Earth's sky. But something strange is happening this time. Halley is vanishing into thin air! Could this be the work of a black hole, or is there a new mystery waiting to be uncovered? It's up to our heroes to find out and ensure the comet returns safely to its path.

Through their adventures, the Sentinels will travel to distant galaxies, dive into the heart of stars, and dance on the rings of Saturn. But it's not all just space walks and rocket rides; they'll learn the value of teamwork, the power of friendship, and the importance of protecting our universe, both the known and the mysterious.

As you turn these pages, you too will explore the marvels of our universe—from the smallest particles in space dust to the massive majesty of black holes. You'll discover how the moon controls the tides, why the sun is essential for life on Earth, and what really happens when a shooting star zooms through the night sky.

So, get ready to unlock the secrets of the cosmos with the Starlight Sentinels. Together, we'll embark on a stellar journey across the universe. Who knows? Maybe you'll be inspired to become a sentinel of the stars too!

The Night Sky Awakens

As the sun dips below the horizon and the first twinkles of light start to appear in the evening sky, something magical happens. The night sky awakens, and with it, the Starlight Sentinels begin their watch. These aren't ordinary kids; they're a team of young guardians from all around the world, chosen to explore and protect the mysteries of our universe.

Imagine a group of friends, just like you and the kids at your school, but with a secret mission to keep the stars shining brightly and the planets spinning smoothly. There's Leo from Brazil, Jin from Korea, Sarah from Kenya, Amir from Egypt, and Mia from Canada. Each has a special love for the stars and a unique talent that helps them on their cosmic adventures.

Tonight, as the Sentinels gather at their secret observatory high atop the tallest mountain, they're looking up at the same sky you see. But what exactly are they looking at? What makes up our beautiful night sky? Well, let's join them and find out!

First, there are the stars. These glowing balls of gas are just like our sun, but much farther away. Some are bigger, some are smaller, and they all twinkle because their light has to travel through Earth's wobbly atmosphere to reach our eyes. When you look up at the night sky, you're seeing thousands of stars, each one a distant sun in its own right.

Next, there are the planets. Unlike stars, which produce their own light, planets like Earth, Mars, and Jupiter reflect the light of the sun. They don't twinkle as stars do; they shine steadily. With a telescope or even a quality pair of binoculars, you can observe some of their details. Jupiter, for instance, has big storms like the Great Red Spot, and Saturn has those amazing rings!

But that's not all. Sprinkled across the sky are patterns of stars called constellations. People long ago imagined these patterns as pictures and gave them names. For example, if you find three stars close together in a line during winter, you've spotted Orion's Belt, part of the hunter Orion. Each constellation has its own story and history, linking us to the ancient people who first named them.

As Leo points to a bright star with his laser pointer, Jin uses her tablet to show how stars are born and how they die. It's like a stellar nursery up there, where stars start from clouds of dust and gas. Sarah sketches quick drawings of the constellations they observe, while Amir calculates their distances from Earth.

Mia, with her notebook, writes down their findings and also notes how different cultures around the world view the same stars.

"Our mission," Leo explains, "is to learn as much as we can about this vast universe and help everyone on Earth appreciate how amazing it is."

As they set up their telescopes and get ready for a night of exploration, the Sentinels are not just watching the stars—they're connecting with the entire universe. And as you close this chapter and look up at your own night sky, remember that you're a part of this grand, cosmic dance too. Maybe, just like the Starlight Sentinels, you'll find your own way to watch over and explore our wonderful universe.

Guardians of the Moon

One crisp, clear evening, as the Starlight Sentinels gathered at their observatory, they prepared for a very special mission—a journey to understand the Moon, Earth's closest neighbor in space. Tonight, they were not just star watchers; they were moon guardians, ready to unravel the mysteries of the lunar surface and its effects on our planet.

Are you aware that the Moon is the sole natural satellite orbiting Earth?" Mia asked, setting up her telescope to get a better view. "It's like Earth's closest friend in space, always present and continually changing through what we call lunar phases.

As the kids adjusted their telescopes, Jin explained these phases. "Like the planets, the Moon doesn't produce its own light. It looks different to us from Earth because it orbits around us, and the Sun lights up different parts of it. This is why we see it change from a tiny sliver to a full circle and back again."

The Sentinels watched intently through their telescopes, observing the Moon's current phase—a first quarter moon.

Half of it was brilliantly lit while the other half disappeared into the shadow. ""It takes about 29.5 days for the Moon to cycle through all its phases, from new Moon to full Moon and back again," Sarah wrote in her journal.

Next, Amir began to talk about the Moon's effects on Earth. "The Moon is really important for Earth. Its gravity pulls on our oceans and causes high and low tides. If you've ever been to the beach and noticed the water coming up higher on the shore, that's high tide, and it's caused by the Moon!"

While they marveled at these scientific facts, Leo brought up another fascinating aspect of the Moon—its role in myths and stories from different cultures. “People all over the world have looked up at the Moon and imagined all sorts of things. Some saw a man in the Moon, others a rabbit, and some even believed it was a powerful god or goddess!”

Mia chimed in with her favorite moon myth. “In Chinese culture, there’s a legend about a woman named Chang’e who drank an elixir and floated up to the Moon, where she became a moon goddess.” They celebrate the Mid-Autumn Festival in her honor with mooncakes and lanterns!”

Sarah shared a story from African folklore about the Moon and the Sun. ““In some African myths, the Moon and the Sun were close friends who shared the sky." But one day, they argued, and now, the Sun spends the day in the sky, while the Moon takes over at night."

As the night deepened and more stars appeared, the Sentinels realized how these stories and scientific facts made the Moon even more special. It was not just a celestial body orbiting Earth; it was a character in humanity's greatest stories, stirring the imaginations of people for thousands of years.

As they packed up their equipment, the Starlight Sentinels felt a deeper connection to the Moon than ever before. They had explored its scientific mysteries and delved into its mythical stories, truly becoming guardians of the Moon. And just like the Moon connects the tides of the seas, it connected the Sentinels from across the world under one sky.

Solar Sentinels

One sunny morning, the Starlight Sentinels were buzzing with excitement as they prepared for a blazing new adventure—exploring the Sun, the heart of our solar system and the source of all life on Earth. Today, they would transform into Solar Sentinels, guardians of the sun's secrets and protectors of its mighty power.

“Okay, team,” Leo announced, pointing to a large poster of the solar system, “the Sun is not just another star; it’s our star and it holds everything together with its gravity. Without it, life on Earth wouldn’t exist.

As they gathered around Leo, Jin pulled up an app on her tablet that simulated the solar system. ““The Sun sits at the center of our solar system, with everything, including Earth, orbiting around it,” she explained, pointing to the paths of the planets.

Sarah, always curious about the details, added, “And it’s huge! Imagine that!” Her eyes widened with the thought.

Amir, who had a passion for all things technical, was the next to speak.It’s always working, turning hydrogen into helium through nuclear fusion, which releases a tremendous amount of energy. This energy travels to Earth as sunlight, which takes about eight minutes to reach us."

Mia, with her notebook in hand, was ready to talk about how this sunlight powers life. "That sunlight is not just for keeping us warm and giving us light. It's essential for plants, which use sunlight to make food through a process called photosynthesis. This process is the base of the food chain, supporting all life on Earth."

The Sentinels then focused on another vital topic: solar energy. Jin explained, "Humans have found ways to capture the Sun's energy and turn it into electricity using solar panels. This clean energy can power everything from homes to schools to gadgets like the one I'm using now!"

But their mission also had to cover the dangers associated with the Sun, particularly solar flares. Amir took the lead on this. "Solar flares are sudden bursts of energy on the Sun's surface, releasing immense amounts of power.They can send particles racing towards Earth, which can interfere with communications and even power grids."

Sarah connected this to a recent event. "Remember last year when some of us lost power for a few hours? That happened due to a powerful solar flare impacting Earth's magnetic field!"

As they all nodded, Leo concluded, "That's why part of being Solar Sentinels is understanding both the benefits and the risks of the Sun. We need to respect its power and learn how to protect our planet from its more dangerous outbursts."

Inspired by their new knowledge, the Sentinels spent the rest of the day building models of solar panels and researching ways to improve solar energy usage. They realized that as Solar Sentinels, they had an important role in not only understanding the Sun's power but also in promoting and using solar energy wisely to protect and enhance life on Earth.

As the day ended and the Sun set, casting a warm golden glow, the Starlight Sentinels felt a new connection to the star that lights up their days and sustains their planet, ready to share their knowledge and help make a brighter, cleaner future.

Comet Watch

The night was unusually dark at the observatory, perfect for a special event—the Starlight Sentinels were hosting their first Comet Watch! Tonight, they would delve into the mysterious and spectacular world of comets, those icy voyagers of the solar system that have fascinated humans for centuries.

As the young guardians set up their telescopes, Mia began the evening with an introduction. “Comets are like cosmic snowballs, made up of ice, dust, and rocky material.”As they orbit the Sun, they heat up and release gases and dust, creating a glowing coma and sometimes a tail that stretches for millions of miles!”

Jin, with her tablet in hand, showed a simulation of a comet’s orbit. “Most comets have long, elliptical orbits. They spend most of their time far from the Sun and only come close every now and then. That’s when we can see them from Earth.”

Amir, always eager to connect the dots, chimed in, “That’s right, and it’s not just their beauty that makes comets so interesting. They're also considered to be ancient leftovers of the solar system formation process, giving us clues about how our planet and others came to be."

Leo was ready with stories of famous comets throughout history. "One of the most well-known comets is Halley's Comet, People around the world have recorded its visits for centuries. The last time it was here was in 1986, and it'll be back in 2061."

Sarah added, "There's also Comet Hale-Bopp, which was incredibly bright and visible to the naked eye for 18 months in 1997." It was one of the most observed comets of the 20th century!"

As the night progressed, Mia discussed the cultural impact of comets. "Different cultures have seen comets as omens. Some thought they brought bad luck or disasters, while others saw them as messengers bringing important news from the gods."

The highlight of the night was when a real comet, Comet Encke, made a brief appearance in the sky. The Sentinels used their telescopes to observe it, and Jin managed to take some pictures with her camera attached to her telescope.

"Look at the tail of Comet Encke!" exclaimed Sarah, pointing at the telescope's digital screen."It's astonishing how the tail always points away from the Sun, no matter which way the comet is moving." That's because the solar wind blows the dust and gases away from the Sun."

Amir had set up a special experiment to show how a comet's tail forms. Using a small model comet made from dry ice and other materials, he demonstrated how the sublimation of dry ice mimics the jet of gases that form a comet's tail. "This is a small-scale version of what happens when a comet gets close to the Sun," he explained.

As the event came to a close, Leo reflected on the evening. "Comet Watch not only "Comet Watch not only taught us about the scientific significance of comets but also how they link us to history and culture." These icy visitors from the distant parts of our solar system really do have a lot to teach us."

Inspired by the night's discoveries, the Starlight Sentinels were more eager than ever to continue their celestial explorations, knowing that every point of light in the sky has a story to tell.

Meteor Shower Shields

On a cool, clear night, the Starlight Sentinels were preparing for one of the most dazzling events in the sky—a meteor shower. Tonight, not only would they witness this spectacular show, but they would also learn all about meteors, meteoroids, and meteorites—pieces of the cosmos that visit our planet in a brilliant blaze.

"Meteors are fascinating," began Leo as he set up a viewing area with blankets and hot cocoa for his friends"When tiny particles of dust and rock from space enter Earth's atmosphere and burn up, we see them as shooting stars or meteors. Most are no larger than a grain of sand!"

Mia, who had brought her new astronomy book, added, "Those bits are called meteoroids when they're out in space. Once they hit Earth's atmosphere and start to burn up, we call them meteors. And if any parts of them manage to reach the ground, those pieces are called meteorites."

Sarah was particularly excited about the night's event. "And tonight, we'll witness the Perseids, one of the most well-known meteor showers." It happens every year when Earth passes through the trail of debris left by Comet Swift-Tuttle."

As the sky darkened, Jin used her tablet to show a simulation of how meteor showers occur. "As Earth passes through the comet's debris, those tiny pieces collide with our atmosphere at high speeds, creating the beautiful light streaks we'll see tonight."

Amir, always looking for a practical application, had set up a camera with a time-lapse function. "I'm going to capture our meteor shower so we can study the different sizes and brightness of the meteors. Maybe we can even catch a fireball!"

The excitement built as the first meteors began to streak across the sky. Each Sentinel took turns using binoculars and telescopes to get a closer look, while Mia noted the time and duration of each significant streak.

Leo shared a helpful tip with the group, "If you follow the paths of the meteors, they all seem to originate from the same point in the sky, known as the radiant.", called the radiant. For the Perseids, it's near the constellation Perseus, which is how the shower got its name."

As they watched, Sarah discussed how people used to view meteor showers. "In ancient times, people believed these were actual stars falling from the sky."

They often associated them with important life events or omens."

The night was not just about watching but learning too. Jin had a small experiment ready. ""This metal plate covered in flour represents the surface of the Ea rth."These pebbles are our meteoroids. Watch what happens when I drop them in," she explained, simulating the impact craters formed by meteorites. The kids could see the small craters in the flour, giving them a hands-on understanding of how meteorites impact Earth.

As the night turned to early morning and the last of the meteors faded, the Sentinels felt a deep sense of wonder and a greater connection to their planet and the universe. They had not only observed a beautiful natural phenomenon but had gained knowledge that transformed tiny streaks of light into meaningful celestial events.

Filled with new insights and warmed by their hot cocoa, the Sentinels wrapped up their meteor watch, already looking forward to their next cosmic adventure. As they packed up, Amir looked up at the fading stars and mused, “It’s incredible to think that we’re not just spectators but part of this vast, interconnected universe.”

Star Patterns

The observatory was abuzz with excitement tonight as the Starlight Sentinels prepared for a special event: a constellation quest! Tonight wasn't just about looking at stars; it was about connecting the dots and discovering the stories they tell.

"Each constellation is like a puzzle," Leo explained as he handed out star maps to his friends. In the past, people gazed at the stars and saw patterns, imagining them as heroes, animals, or objects from their legends and daily lives.

As darkness enveloped the sky, Mia pointed her laser at a group of bright stars. “Let’s Let’s begin with one of the most well-known constellations, Orion the Hunter.in a line? That’s Orion’s Belt .The four bright stars surrounding them form the outline of his body.”Jin, with her tablet ready, pulled up an image of Orion from different cultures. “In “In Greek mythology, Orion was a powerful hunter, while in Egyptian culture, the stars of Orion were linked to Osiris, the god of the afterlife.”Different cultures saw the same stars but told different stories.”

The Sentinels used their telescopes to trace the stars of Orion, and Sarah added, "The two brightest stars, Betelgeuse and Rigel, represent Orion's shoulder and foot. Betelgeuse is actually a red supergiant, which means it's really big and old."

Amir, who loved to delve deeper into the history, shared, "Constellations also helped ancient sailors navigate the seas. For instance, sailors used the North Star, Polaris, which is part of the Little Dipper, to find their way north."

As the night progressed, the team explored more constellations. Leo guided them to Leo pointed them toward another group of stars. "This is the Big Dipper, a part of the larger constellation

Ursa Major, the Great Bear."But did you know that in Hindu mythology, these stars are the seven great sages, the Saptarishi?"

Mia, fascinated by the different interpretations, pointed her telescope towards another area. "And there's Cassiopeia! It looks like a big W or M in the sky, depending on its position. Cassiopeia was a queen in Greek mythology who boasted about her unrivaled beauty."

As the Sentinels took turns looking through their telescopes, Jin pulled up an interactive star map on her tablet. "Let's find Scorpius. It's supposed to be a scorpion, "It's meant to represent a scorpion, and according to Greek legends, it's the scorpion that stung Orion."

Sarah, who had been sketching the constellations in her notebook, mused, "It's amazing how these stars have connected people across time and space. They're the same stars, but the stories they inspire are as vast as the sky itself."

To wrap up their quest, Amir set up a small projector to display the night sky indoors. "Let's create our own constellation stories," he suggested. The Sentinels each chose different stars and invented new constellations with their own modern legends, drawing them out and sharing their tales.

As the night drew to a close, Leo reflected on their adventures. "Whether they're Tonight, we added our own stories to the celestial tapestry, and that's pretty stellar!"

Galactic Explorers

Today was no ordinary day at the observatory; the Starlight Sentinels were preparing for an imaginary journey unlike any other—a voyage across the galaxies! With star maps in hand and imaginations ready to soar, they embarked on an adventure to explore the Milky Way and beyond, learning about the vast communities of stars and planets that make up galaxies.

"Think of galaxies as enormous cities of stars," Leo began, gesturing toward a beautifully illustrated poster of the Milky Way. "Our solar system is just one tiny neighborhood in this vast star-filled city." And the Milky Way is just one of billions of galaxies in the universe!"

Mia, always keen to add detail, chimed in, "Our galaxy is a spiral galaxy, which means it has these sweeping arms that stretch out from the center, kind of like a giant pinwheel in space. The center, or the galactic core, is super bright because it's packed with stars!"

Amir, who had been setting up the computer simulation, invited everyone to join him. "Let's start our journey right here at home and zoom out to see where we are in the Milky Way." The screen displayed a stunning visualization of their journey from Earth, past the outer planets, and beyond, into the spiraling arms of the Milky Way.

"Notice how we move from our local neighborhood, past other solar systems, and through clouds of gas and dust, all swirling around the galactic center," explained Jin, guiding the simulation with expert clicks.

The journey didn't end there. Sarah was ready to take them further. "Now, let's visit some other galaxies. Each one is unique, like a city with its own layout and personality." The screen now showed a variety of galaxies: spirals with graceful arms, elliptical galaxies that were more rounded and diffuse, and irregular galaxies that didn't have any clear shape at all.

Leo added, "These different shapes tell us about the life of a galaxy—what it's been through, how old it might be, and even its future. For example, when galaxies collide, they can merge and change shape, creating entirely new types of galaxies!"

As they explored an animation of two galaxies colliding and merging into one, Mia discussed the implications. "These cosmic events aren't just spectacular; they're also creative forces. New stars can form from the gas and dust stirred up by the merging of galaxies."

To give a sense of scale and interaction, Jin introduced a concept. "Imagine if alien astronomers in a galaxy far away were looking at us right now through their telescopes. They might see the Milky Way as just a small part of a massive cluster of galaxies, all interacting and moving through space together."

The session concluded with a hands-on activity. Each Sentinel created a simple model of different galaxy types using swirling patterns of glitter and paint on black paper. This craft helped reinforce the shapes and structures of galaxies they had learned about.

As they cleaned up, Sarah reflected on the day's adventures. "It's incredible to think about how vast the universe is, and yet, in some ways, it's all connected. Our galaxy, our home, is just one part of this enormous cosmic tapestry."

With minds full of new cosmic knowledge and hearts inspired by the wonders of the universe, the Starlight Sentinels looked forward to their next celestial adventure, ready to explore more mysteries of the cosmos.

Black Hole Mystery

Tonight at the observatory, the Starlight Sentinels were gearing up for one of their most thrilling adventures yet: unraveling the mystery of black holes. These cosmic enigmas, known for their incredible gravity from which not even light can escape, had always sparked the curiosity of our young explorers.

"Black holes sound like something from a science fiction movie, but they're very real," Leo began, as he adjusted the projector to display a swirling animation of a black hole. "They form from the remnants of massive stars that have collapsed under their own gravity."

As the animation showed a star collapsing and shrinking into an incredibly dense point, Mia explained further. "When a really big star uses up all its fuel, it can no longer support its own weight. It collapses and, if it's big enough, turns into a black hole. It's like squeezing Earth into a marble!"

Jin, who had been reading up on black holes, added, "The point where the star collapses is called the singularity, and the surrounding area where gravity is so strong that light can't escape is known as the event horizon. It's like the point of no return."

To illustrate, Amir conducted a simple experiment with a stretchy fabric held up by a ring and a heavy ball placed in the center to represent the black hole. "Imagine this fabric is space-time. When we put the ball, which represents a black hole, in the middle, you can see how it bends the fabric around it. That's what black holes do to space!"

Sarah, always interested in the broader implications, chimed in. "This warping of space also affects time. Near a black hole, time actually slows down because of the intense gravity. It's a phenomenon predicted by Einstein's theory of relativity."

The Sentinels were fascinated. Mia posed a thoughtful question, "If someone could travel close to a black hole and then return, they might find that much more time has passed on Earth than for them. It's like time travel into the future!"

Leo pulled up another simulation showing how galaxies might have supermassive black holes at their centers, acting as the anchors. "These supermassive black holes are millions or even billions of times more massive than our Sun, and they might play a role in how galaxies form and evolve."

As the night progressed, the Sentinels used the observatory's telescope, equipped with special filters, to look at areas in space where astronomers believe black holes exist, near the centers of galaxies and in regions marked by high-energy X-ray emissions.

"Even though we can't see black holes directly because no light escapes from them, we can detect the effects they have on the stars and gas around them," explained Jin as she adjusted the telescope.

To conclude their adventure, the group discussed the possibilities of what might lie beyond the event horizon of a black hole, though it remains one of the greatest mysteries in modern science.

With minds full of wonder, the Starlight Sentinels wrapped up their night with a deeper appreciation of one of the universe's most mysterious phenomena. Each Sentinel felt a mix of awe and inspiration, realizing that space holds endless mysteries yet to be solved.

THE AURORA PHENOMENON

The Starlight Sentinels had a special nighttime mission at the observatory—exploring the mesmerizing dance of the Northern and Southern Lights, known scientifically as the aurora borealis and aurora australis. Tonight, they would learn how the Sun's energy creates one of Earth's most spectacular natural light shows.

"As we settle in, let's start with what causes these beautiful lights," Leo began, as he projected images of colorful auroras on the screen. "The story of auroras begins with the Sun, over 93 million miles away from us."

Mia took over with a smile, "The Sun is always active, and sometimes it sends out huge bursts of solar wind.These are streams of charged particles, primarily electrons and protons, that flow outward into space.

Amir, ready with a model of the Earth and a fan, illustrated this concept. "Imagine this fan is the Sun, and the air it blows represents solar wind. When these charged particles from the solar wind reach Earth, they meet our planet's magnetic field."

Jin added, "Earth's magnetic field is like a protective shield. It stretches far into space and guides the solar wind particles towards the poles." She used magnets and iron filings to show how magnetic lines of force worked, directing the filings to the ends of the magnet, simulating the particles' journey to the poles.

"As these charged particles from the solar wind travel along Earth's magnetic field lines, they collide with gases in our atmosphere, like oxygen and nitrogen," Sarah explained, switching the slides to show how these collisions emit light. "Different gases emit different colors when they're excited. Oxygen gives off green and red light, while nitrogen produces blue and purple hues."

Leo dimmed the lights to enhance the colorful images of auroras flickering across the screen. "These lights can form in many patterns, like curtains, rays, spirals, and even dynamic shapes that seem to dance across the sky. This is what makes the aurora one of nature's most beautiful displays."

The group then discussed how auroras are not just beautiful but also scientifically significant. "Auroras help scientists study the Earth's atmosphere and magnetic field. They can also tell us more about solar activity and how it affects our planet," Mia noted, emphasizing the broader impacts of these stunning natural events.

To wrap up, the Sentinels engaged in a hands-on activity, using phosphorescent materials and UV lights to create their own mini auroras. “Although we can’t replicate the exact process of the aurora, this activity gives us a feel for how dynamic and vibrant these lights can be,” Amir said as everyone admired their glowing creations.

The chapter concluded with the Sentinels setting up their next observation night, hoping to catch a glimpse of an aurora themselves. “Though we may not see an aurora tonight, just knowing the science behind them makes the sky seem even more fascinating,” Sarah reflected, capturing the sentiment of the whole group.

Their exploration of the aurora phenomenon not only broadened their understanding of Earth's interaction with solar activity but also deepened their appreciation for the natural wonders of their home planet.

Beyond the Stars

The Starlight Sentinels gathered for one final adventure in their series, aiming their gaze far beyond the familiar stars and galaxies, into the depths of the unknown—the very edge of the universe. Tonight, they would explore the outer limits of our cosmic understanding and dream about the future of space exploration.

"As we look up at the night sky, we're seeing only a small part of the universe. The observable universe includes everything we can see from Earth, but there's so much more beyond that," Leo began, setting the stage for an evening of wonder and curiosity.

Mia, always eager to dive into details, added, "The observable universe is like a bubble around us, about 93 billion light-years in diameter. Beyond that, it's hard to know for sure what exists because the light from there hasn't reached us yet."

Jin took over with a sparkle in her eye, "And it's expanding! The universe is getting bigger every moment, which means the farthest edges are moving away from us faster than the speed of light. That makes them impossible to see with current technology."

Amir, flipping through a book on cosmology, shared an intriguing thought, "Some scientists speculate that beyond our observable universe, there might be other 'universes' with different laws of physics.

Sarah, intrigued by these ideas, wondered aloud, "What does this mean for the future of space exploration?" She switched the projector to display upcoming space missions.

"The future of space exploration looks brighter than ever," Leo responded. "Agencies like NASA, ESA, and private companies are planning missions further into space. For example, the James Webb Space Telescope, which will be able to look back in time to see the first galaxies that formed after the Big Bang."

Mia highlighted another ambitious project, "There's also talk about the Artemis program, which aims to return humans to the Moon and eventually to Mars. These missions will help us test technologies for living and working on other planets."

As the conversation turned to technology, Jin mentioned newer propulsion technologies that might one day take us to the stars. "Scientists are working on things like ion thrusters and nuclear propulsion, which could drastically reduce travel time to distant planets and maybe even to other star systems."

The Sentinels then engaged in a group activity, creating a timeline of past and future space missions on a large poster. Each Sentinel added a mission, noting its significance and how it pushed the boundaries of what humanity could achieve in space.

Amir summed up the session with a thoughtful note, "Exploring space teaches us not just about the universe, but also about our place within it. It shows us that we're part of a much larger cosmos and inspires us to keep reaching out into the unknown."

As they packed up for the night, the Starlight Sentinels felt a mix of awe and excitement about the future. The universe was vast, and its mysteries were waiting to be unlocked. With eyes full of stars and hearts full of dreams, they left the observatory, knowing that their journey of discovery was just beginning.

Final Voyage

As our adventure with the Starlight Sentinels comes to an end, one thing is certain: the wonders of the universe are endless, and the journey of discovery is just beginning. Together, we've explored the stars, planets, moons, and galaxies, learning how the universe works and what makes our place in it so special.

We've seen how stars are born, how they shine, and how they eventually fade away. We've followed comets as they zip through space, watched meteor showers light up the night sky, and marveled at the glowing auroras that dance above the Earth. We've even ventured into the unknown, where black holes bend space and time, and the edge of the universe stretches far beyond what we can see.

Through it all, the Starlight Sentinels have shown us that curiosity, teamwork, and a love for learning are the keys to understanding the cosmos. But the story doesn't end here. The night sky is filled with mysteries still waiting to be uncovered, and new adventures are always just a glance at the stars away.

So, the next time you look up at the sky, remember: you are part of this vast, amazing universe. Whether you're spotting a constellation, watching the Moon, or dreaming of far-off galaxies, you're joining the explorers who have looked up at the stars for centuries. And who knows? Maybe one day, you'll be the one to make the next big discovery!

The universe is full of possibilities, and your journey is just beginning. Keep asking questions, keep exploring, and never stop reaching for the stars.

About the Author

Hey there, I'm Sage Woods. I've been told that I am a captivating children's author known for my enchanting stories like Aurora's Allies ,Starlight Sentinels, Comet Riders, Moonlight Guardians and Galaxy Guardians, which are all part of the "Sky Explorers Teeney Tiny Guidebook Series"

But really I just love to write and share my passion for the wonders of the night sky with everyone I meet.

Growing up with four equally creative sisters—Wilhelmina, River, Willow, and Raven—I was always surrounded by a love for storytelling and adventure. Whether it's gazing at the night sky with my beloved dogs and cats or weaving tales that transport young readers to the stars, I find endless inspiration in the magic of the universe. I feel that my books reflect my deep connection to the cosmos, and invite children to explore the mysteries of the night and beyond.

www.ingramcontent.com/pod-product-compliance
Lightning Source LLC
LaVergne TN
LVHW010119170826
845678LV00012B/2494

9781991306777